Shining Mountains

The Splendour of Banff National Park

Shining Mountains

The Splendour of Banff National Park

Published by

Whitecap Books Ltd.
2229 Jefferson Ave.,
West Vancouver, B.C.
V7V 2A9

First Edition

ISBN 0-920620-11-6 (paperback)
ISBN 0-920620-12-4 (hardcover)

Printed in Canada

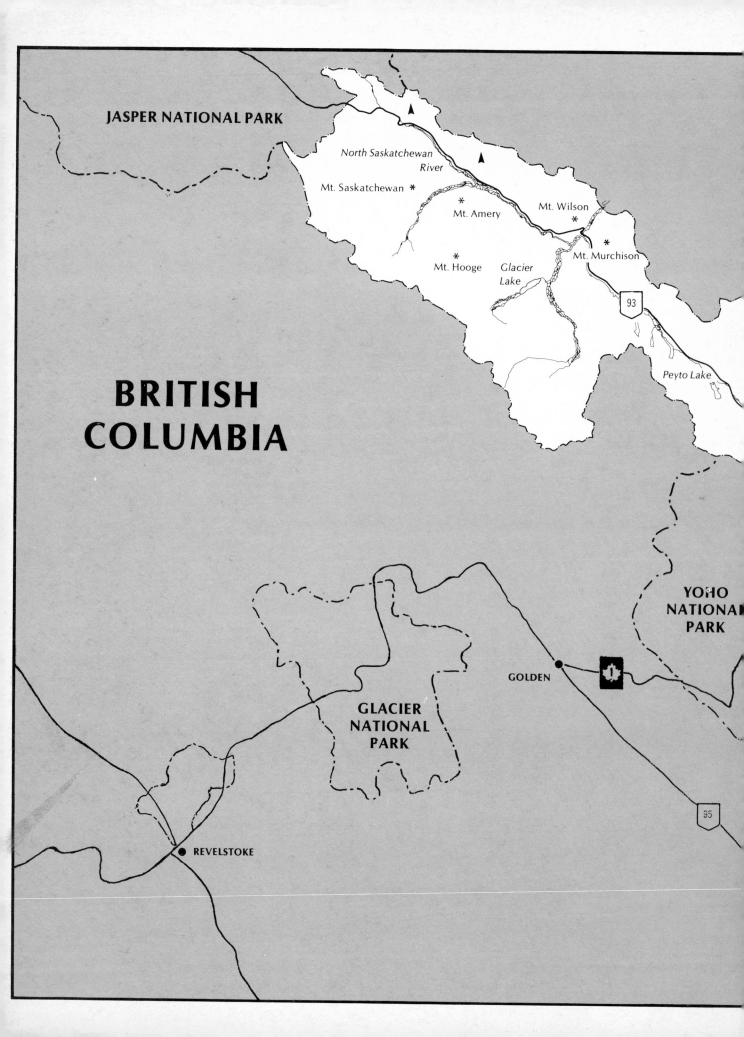

JASPER NATIONAL PARK

North Saskatchewan River

Mt. Saskatchewan ✳

✳
Mt. Amery

Mt. Wilson
✳

✳
Mt. Hooge

Glacier Lake

Mt. Murchison
✳

93

Peyto Lake

BRITISH COLUMBIA

YOHO
NATIONAL
PARK

GOLDEN ●
1

GLACIER
NATIONAL
PARK

95

● REVELSTOKE

BANFF NATIONAL PARK
6640 Sq. Km./2,564 Sq. Miles

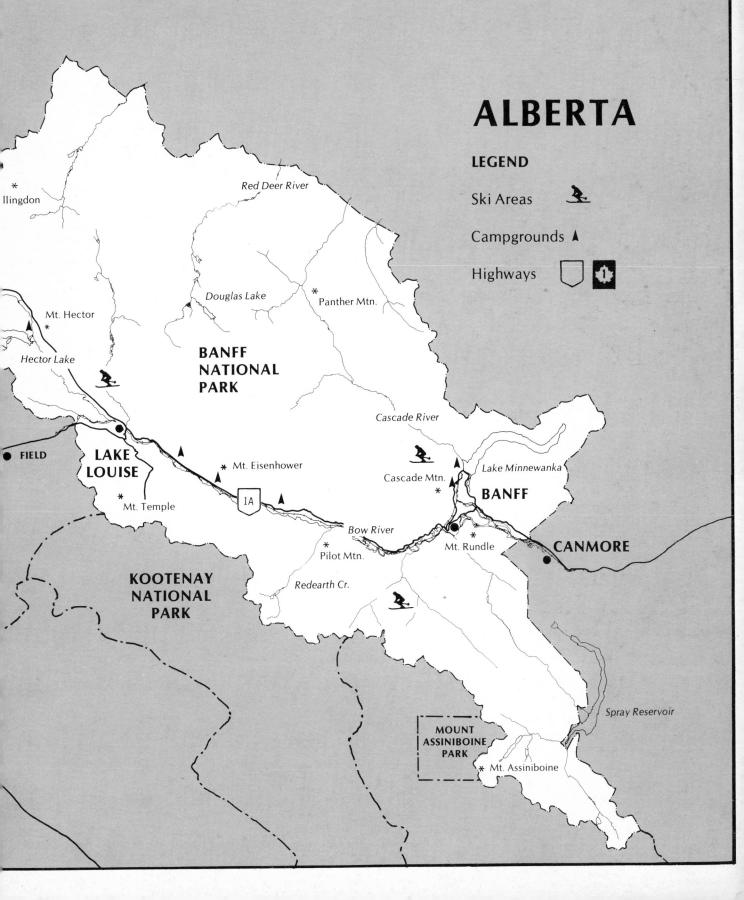

ALBERTA

LEGEND

Ski Areas

Campgrounds ▲

Highways

*Ilingdon

*Red Deer River

*Douglas Lake

*Panther Mtn.

Mt. Hector
*

Hector Lake

**BANFF
NATIONAL
PARK**

Cascade River

FIELD

**LAKE
LOUISE**

*Mt. Eisenhower

Cascade Mtn.
*

Lake Minnewanka

BANFF

*Mt. Temple

IA

Bow River

CANMORE

*Pilot Mtn.

Mt. Rundle

**KOOTENAY
NATIONAL
PARK**

Redearth Cr.

Spray Reservoir

**MOUNT
ASSINIBOINE
PARK**

*Mt. Assiniboine

Photo Credits

Jan Krejcik — Front cover, page 9, page 10, page 12 (above), page 15 (above), pages 16 and 17, page 18, page 19, page 21, page 22, page 23 (below right), pages 34 and 35, page 38, page 39 (above), page 41, page 45 (below), page 46 (below), page 47, page 49, page 52 (above right), back cover.

Anders Lenes — Page 11 (above), page 13 (below), page 14 (above), page 20 (above and below), page 23 (above left), page 27 (above), page 30 (above), page 42 (below), page 43 (above), page 45 (above), page 48 (below left and right), page 51 (above), page 52 (above left), page 55.

Simon Hoyle — Page 11 (below), page 14 (below), page 26, page 31, page 42 (above), page 44, page 50 (above).

Jean Finley — Page 39 (below).

J. A. Kraulis — Page 15 (below), page 23 (below left), page 24, page 27 (below), page 30 (below), page 43 (below), page 50 (below).

Raymond Jotterand — Page 23 (above right), page 51 (below), page 53.

Duncan McDougall — Page 48 (above left), page 52 (below), page 54.

Pat Morrow — Page 46 (above).

Introduction

There's a place in the Canadian Rockies where the air is washed cold and clean by summer storms. As the clouds lift, the traveller stands in wonder, encircled by great mountains shining in the sun. The foreground of forested slopes gives way to a bewildering series of horizons - rocky ridges, crags, and high peaks hung with snow.

The summer sun falls through stands of lodgepole pine, warming the scented air. The Bow River streams in a swell of blue-green water across the floor of the valley before plunging in a foamy torrent over Bow Falls.

A little above the falls sits Banff, a bustling centre welcoming visitors from all over the world. Both the mainline of the Canadian Pacific Railway and the Trans-Canada Highway pass through the Bow Valley and bring travellers spilling into the town. For some, Banff is the destination. For many more, it is the starting point. From here, visitors by car and bus travel the scenic parkways to Lake Louise and Jasper. Others abandon the highways to explore the quiet mountain trails.

The earliest visitors to the Banff area were the Indians, those from the east coming by way of the Ghost River and Lake Minnewanka. Old campfires near the water's edge and the trails of hunters and horses were all that marked their route. Here and there in remote canyons the Indians painted the rocks, perhaps asking a blessing on the hunt. It was Indians who later guided the whites into the wilderness of the mountains or 'Arsinee Watchee', the 'Rock Hills' spoken of to Anthony Henday and seen by him from a distance in 1754.

The Rockies were first crossed in the late eighteenth century by Howse and Athabasca passes. White men did not reach the Banff area until 1841 when Sir George Simpson, Governor of the Hudson's Bay Company arrived with his party. He was determined to be the first man to circle the globe east to west by land. The mountains near Banff only briefly stood in his way. A driven man, he must have been irritated when the mountains slowed his usual pace of sixty horseback miles a day. They crossed the Bow River in

August, 1841 and the next day continued to the Continental Divide and Simpson Pass near today's Sunshine ski area. There Simpson was suddenly reminded of Scotland as he saw the red and white mountain heather which still spreads over the meadows.

Before leaving England on this world tour, Governor Simpson had been in London during meetings of Hudson's Bay Committee and the Wesleyan Missionary Society. The following year three young Englishmen were assigned work in the Company's Territory. One of these was Robert Terrill Rundle whose name was later given by Hector to the 'tilted' mountain southeast of Banff.

Rundle's journal records that he preached on the shores of Lake Minnewanka. In the evening a full moon rose over the mountains, lighting the water he called 'the most interesting lake I ever saw.' Rundle preferred to visit the Indians in their own camps rather than in the forts, and always found them an hospitable people. His interest in the language and customs of the Indians is found in his journal, the first written record of the area by a white man not involved in the fur trade.

In 1858 a doctor and geologist, Dr. James Hector entered the mountains, explored a large portion of today's mountain national parks and named many of its finest features including the famous Kicking Horse River in Yoho National Park. Hector was one of the four scientists of the British Palliser Expedition of 1857 - 1860. The report and map published on their return to Britian was the first full description of the area now known as Western Canada. Until then the region was described only in terms of the fur trade, not in terms of possible agriculture, settlement and political status.

In 1859 the first genuine tourist visited Banff, the somewhat eccentric adventurer James Carnegie, the 9th Earl of Southesk. Beginning his trip in the eastern valleys of today's Jasper National Park, he hoped to find good hunting and the climate and exercise that would restore his health. So exhausting was the trip, and so late in the season, that the 'health cure' was almost fatal. But even in the roughest camps he did not abandon his evening pleasure. After one less that perfect supper of mountain goat 'tougher and drier fare I never fed on...' he retired to his tent to read Romeo and Juliet. As he left the mountains for flatter land to the east he wrote: 'On the 1st of September I entered the mountains with joy, on the 1st of October I leave them with greater joy.'

The Palliser Expedition crossed three different passes in the Rockies but decided none of them was practicable as a route to the coast. By 1871 the pressure was on to locate a feasible crossing, for in that year British Columbia joined Confederation. By the terms of this union, the Canadian Government would within ten years build a railroad to connect the west coast to the Atlantic seaboard. Such a promise seemed absurd as preliminary surveys took several years and vast amounts of money. The early surveyors worked under tremendous difficulties, hauling heavy instruments to mountaintops or standing knee-deep in mud in the valley bottoms. They should be honoured both as early mountaineers and skilled bushwhackers.

Soon the railroad project was handed over to the private company whose name is a by-word on this continent, the Canadian Pacific Railway. By 1883 the actual construction of the line had brought numbers of tie-cutters and navvies into the area and the settlement of Siding 29 sprang up. This cluster of tents and log cabins was at the foot of the Indians' 'Mountain where the water falls', today called Cascade Mountain. The same waterfall Sir George Simpson called 'The Spout' still pours down the cliffs.

(Right:) The Banff Springs Hotel sits amid the natural beauty of The Rockies. When it was originally built in the 1880's it transformed a wilderness, and the town of Banff.

Preceding pages (left:) Pilot Mountain 2954m (9690 ft.) with Redearth Creek in the foreground. (Right above:) Mushrooms in the early morning. (Right below:) The Monarch 2905m (9528 ft.) makes a beautiful backdrop for skiers at the Sunshine ski area.

(Opposite:) Fall foliage. (Left:) A black Bear enjoys the spring sun. This species is often sighted in the developed and wilderness areas. (Below:) The Red Squirrel is common throughout Canada. This hardy little mammal can be seen in many areas of the park.

Following pages; (Left above:) Cascade Mountain 2998m (9836 ft.) as seen from Banff Avenue in Banff. (Left below:) A canoe trip in summer. (Right above:) The Canadian Pacific railway between Banff and Lake Louise. (Right below:) Mount Hungerbee 3493m (11,457 ft.) and Paradise Valley.

(Pages 16 and 17:) The Vermilion Lakes near Banff are a popular hiking area. The lakes are accessible on foot from the Trans-Canada Highway, or from Banff. They are also accessible by canoe along the Bow River. In the background from left to right are Mount Inglismaldie 2,966m (9,725 ft.), Mount Girouard 2,996m (9,825 ft.), and Mount Peechee 2,936m (9,625 ft.).

Preceding pages (Left:) Mount Temple 3548m (11,636 ft.) looms majestically across the Bow River. (Right:) A golden-mantled ground squirrel.

(Opposite:) Fairview Mountain 2747m (9,011 ft.) as seen from the Trans-Canada Highway near Lake Louise. (Right:) The Mountain Goat lives in rocky areas at and above the timber line. (Below:) The vivid reds of the Canadian fall.

(Opposite:) Hoodoos near Banff. These rock formations are caused by years of erosion into cliff faces. (Above:) An Anemone in seed. (Below:) Aspens at the base of Mount Rundle.

(Above:) Mountain climbing is a sport for the more intrepid visitor to Banff National Park. (Below:) Indian Paintbrush in full bloom.

Banff

After construction of the Canadian Pacific Railway began in 1883 prospectors, trappers, and suppliers swelled the population of the company settlement of Siding 29. Timber permits were taken out up and down the valley and coal was mined at Anthracite, the first station east of Siding 29. Meanwhile on the south side of the river on the forested slope below Sulphur Mountain, hotsprings were discovered. The railroad workers would clamber down a treetrunk ladder placed through a natural opening in the top of a cave. After luxuriating in the murky heated depths they struggled up the forty feet to daylight. The certain tourist attraction of these thermal waters prompted the government to ease out several claimants to the springs. By Order-in-Council on November 25, 1885 the Banff Hot Springs Reserve of ten square miles around the springs was established. This small preserve of land in its unique mountain setting was the beginning of Canada's national parks system.

The Order-in-council of 1885 kept ten square miles around the Cave Springs 'from sale, or settlement or squatting'. In this way the medicinal benefits of the hot waters would be available for the ailing from across the land. But the splendid backdrop of forest and mountain lured the hale and hearty. Completing the railroad to the west coast nearly crippled the company financially. If the Banff Hot Springs Reserve were attractive to tourists, passenger ticket sales would increase, and both government and railroad would be pleased. The grand future of the town was about to unfold; the new name of Banff honoured the birthplace in Scotland of Donald Smith, then president of the C.P.R.

(Opposite page) A Gray Jay poses on a frosty bough. The Gray or Canada Jay is a large, fluffy, grey bird slightly bigger than a Robin, and is found throughout Banff National Park.

Sometimes known as the Whiskeyjack they can become quite tame, especially around ski areas where many a skier has been relieved of part of his lunch by these audacious birds.

At present the Cave Springs which aroused all this interest, and the Cave and Basin pool are closed. Erosion and humidity have endangered the structure built to enclose the waters. In 1985 however, on the one hundredth anniversary of Banff National Park, the building will be reopened as a centre to interpret the early history of the park.

The well-developed Upper Hot Springs is located on the northeastern slope of Sulphur Mountain. In the early days the steps from the Old Grand View Hotel to the pool were accompanied by a wooden railing trimmed with the crutches of the cured. These touches of a rustic shrine are gone. The modern year-round facilities of the Upper Hot Springs include the outdoor hot pool, plunges, steam rooms and massage. For the mid-winter visitor nothing is quite so satisfying as bobbing in the outdoor hot pool and gazing up through the steam as large snowflakes drift down to melt in the water.

All the hot springs in the area are probably supplied with water originating in Sundance Creek two miles west of the Cave and Basin. Some of this water percolates to a depth of 2500 metres or 8000 feet below the surface where it is heated. Then it rises through fractures in the layers of rock and emerges as hotspring water, bringing with it dissolved salts from the rocks. The return journey of the water is estimated to take about three months.

More than hotsprings interested visiting Members of Parliament in 1886. They proposed enlarging the Reserve to protect the natural beauties of the area. In 1887 some 260 square miles were set aside by Act of Parliament as Rocky Mountains Park.

The idea was strongly supported by Sir William Van Horne, general manager of the C.P.R., who saw tourist gold in the Rockies and in the Selkirk Mountains to the west. By 1886 construction was already underway on two mountain hotels, Mount Stephen House at Field and Glacier House at Rogers Pass.

The rugged splendour of the Banff Springs Hotel was to be exceeded only by the mountains themselves. With its French chateau style and gracious interior the hotel inspired the noble and wealthy of the world as they travelled through the otherwise unrefined western Canada of the day. Royalty, movie stars, business tycoons and artists have strolled the sunlit terrace overlooking the Bow and dined and danced into the night. In recent years most guests have been delegates to conferences or members of bus tours who make full use of the golf course, pool, and tennis courts, or in winter are away all day on the ski slopes. Behind the scenes, hundreds of bustling staff have coped with the intricacies of 'the castle' and more than one generation of university students has laboured in its kitchens and dining rooms.

From near the Upper Hot Springs a footpath leads to the ridge of Sulphur Mountain and a fine view of the Bow Valley and surrounding peaks and ranges. The effortless means to the

Preceding pages (Left:) Members of Canada's cross-country ski team during a practice at the Sunshine ski area. (Right above:) Mount Rundle 2950m (9675 ft.) is a good example of a mountain cut into layered sedimentary rocks. This hugh 'tilted' mountain lies immediately southeast of Banff. (Right below:) A panoramic view of the Selkirk Range in British Columbia as seen from atop Mount Temple.

summit is by the famous Sulphur Mountain Gondola Lift.

The old and new paths of the Bow River are more easily seen from this height. At the end of the last ice age the glacier which had moved down the Bow Valley retreated Water from the glacier flowed through the valley of today's Lake Minnewanka and also streamed around the southern or Bow Falls end of Tunnel Mountain. There the water carved a deeper valley that finally received all the run-off and left the other route dry.

Those glacial times ended as recently as 10,000 years ago. Buth the mountains visible from Sulphur Mountain were formed millions of years before the ice ages. All the mountains in the park are of sedimentary origin. Their rocks were formed when rivers flowing from still older mountains left layers of gravel, sand and mud on the floor of an ancient inland sea. These sediments formed thick layers of limestones and shales about 350 million years ago. Much later, 65 or 70 million years ago, the continental crust began to buckle and fold and the waters receded. The exposed sea floor was bent creating the ridges and crests and structural valleys of the Rockies. Parts of the crust which did not withstand the strain of folding, fractured and tilted, forming mountains such as Rundle. Ice, snow, water and wind erosion have gradually wrought further changes.

A favourite view of Mount Rundle for photographers is from the Vermilion Lakes just west of Banff. These shimmering backwaters of the Bow were formed comparatively recently. The three shallow lakes cover glacial and river deposits overlaid by organic deposits of plant life.

Although the lakes can be reached by road, the more peaceful approach is by canoe up the creeks from the Bow River. When water droplets from a paddle are the only sound, beaver and waterfowl and perhaps the long billed marsh wren can be more easily observed. The rich diversity of plant, animal and bird life makes Vermilion Lakes area unique in the park, an area to be protectively treasured against the pressure of adjacent transportation routes.

As understanding grows of the various components of the park, whatever the eye beholds becomes a subject worthy of meditation: hoodoos above the riverbank, a colony of Columbian ground squirrels, or the star-flowered Solomon's seal beside the trail. Important 'eye-openers' are offered by the Park Naturalists with guided walks in summer, snowshoe and ski tours in winter, and slide-talks and films to round out the programme. The main Information Centre is located on Banff Avenue.

The resources of the Peter Whyte Foundation are also appreciated by visitors and residents alike. Adjacent to the public library, the Archives of the Canadian Rockies preserves the history of the parks in photographs, maps, tape recordings and written accounts. Downstairs the gallery displays the work of local and national artists.

(Left:) Young Mule deer feeding near Lake Minnewanka. Unlike many deer the Mule deer do not usually congregate in herds, although two to four may frequently be found together.

The original Buckskin leather was made by Indians from the tanned hides of Mule deer.

(Below:) Mount Rundle 2950m (9675 ft.) This view is from the Trans-Canada Highway, and the east face of the mountain can be seen in the background. The east face is steeper than the other side which is visible from Banff.

(Right:) The thrill of powder skiing in the Canadian Rockies.

In the serene log building by 'Central Park' the Government Museum displays mounted birds and mammals and geological and botanical specimens collected in the mountain parks.

Across the river in a structure resembling a log fort is a branch of the Glenbow-Alberta Institute, the Luxton Museum, life-like figures in camping and hunting scenes depicting the way of life of the Plains Indians.

Two local events may highlight a summer visit to the town. In July the daily parade by several bands of Plains Indians marks Banff Indian Days. A tipi camp is set up for the week and visitors can watch the singing and dancing.

The Banff Festival of the Arts is held in August at the Banff Centre. The theatres, classrooms and gallery are busy with performances of music, opera, dance and drama, and displays of photography, ceramics, weaving and visual arts.

On the north side of the traffic circle a road leads past the site of Bankhead, an early coal mining town, to the shore of Lake Minnewanka. Boat tours take sightseers to the end of the lake close to Devil's Head mountain and back below the slopes of Mount Inglismaldie.

Two other tranquil drives in the area are the Tunnel Mountain Loop and Mount Norquay from both of which good viewpoints overlook the town and valley.

A car is needed to visit the Buffalo Park since the animals may not be approached on foot. Buffalo have been enclosed inside the park since the 1890's. But the additions to the herd in 1907 were the result of more than a few years' work by Howard Douglas the second Superintendent of the park. He appreciated buffalo as a noble and wild animal and as a tourist attraction.

In Montana, Michel Pablo found himself the sole owner of several hundred animals, a herd built up by himself and his late partner, C.A. Allard. Pablo was anxious for the future of the herd since the Flathead Reserve where they ranged was to be opened up to settlers. The Canadian Government sent Douglas to look over the situation and conduct quiet negotiations. Four years later, and after enormous difficulties in the round-up of animals which will not be driven like cattle, Canada was the owner of 703 plains bison. Most of the animals went to Wainright, Alberta, and were transferred to Elk Island National Park.

Lake Louise

In the summer, hotel staff at Lake Louise swells the resident population to over a thousand. The permanent winter population is only about one hundred and fifty.

Back in the famous winter of 1883-84 some 500 men stayed in roughly made bunkhouses and log shanties. Next spring 12,000 men passed through for the pushing of the line to the Pacific. Holt City, soon after called Laggan, was the C.P.R.'s staging area for Kicking Horse Pass to the west. The work there was slow and dangerous as the mountainside was carved out by hand and a precarious bed made for the steel. The eight-mile drop from Hector to Field stations became known as the 'Big Hill.' With a grade of 232 feet in a mile not surprisingly several engines were lost to the river below.

Timber cutting occurred around Holt City and sawmills screamed from the valley bottom. Much of the wood met the urgent needs of the C.P.R. while some was destined for Canmore just east of Banff where the developing coal mines required stout timbers for shafts and tunnels.

A stream of pack-trains supplied the railhead as it moved westward. One of the packers working for the C.P.R. at this time was Tom Wilson, who later had his own outfitting and guiding business employing Bill Peyto, Jim Simpson, Ralph Edwards and others.

One day in August 1882 Wilson took time out from work in the valley bottom. Curious about the distant rumble of ice-falls he made his way up the densely forested slopes with a Stony Indian companion. The Indian's 'Lake of Little Fishes' is known today around the world as Lake Louise. With the changing light of each hour, and by storm and sun the lake has many moods. These moods escape easy description and bring visitors back year after year to wonder once more.

The colour of Lake Louise and of other lakes in the Rockies is caused by the light reflecting on water containing minute particles in suspension. These particles enter the lake by glacier-fed streams. Kucera's book on the Lake Louise area, Exploring Glaciers and Mountains explains how varying amounts of sediment in water effect light

rays shining through it. When ice leaves the lake in early summer the clear water appears blue. As more suspended particles are added during the summer run-off from the glaciers, the water deepens to green. Tom Wilson first saw the lake in late summer and not surprisingly called it Emerald Lake. The name Lake Louise was given in 1884, probably to honour Princess Louise, the wife of Canada's Governor General, the Marquis of Lorne.

The mountains in the Lake Louise area belong to the Main Ranges of the Rockies. Like the Front Ranges of the Banff area their rock is sedimentary in origin. Folding and fracturing of the layers is typical of the Front Ranges, but in the Main Ranges a gradual raising and dipping of the layers is more common. Great fractures do occur, however, where adjacent bands of sedimentary rocks show 'displacement' of hundreds of feet. These 'normal faults' have occurred where rock has broken under the stress of the earth's crust moving.

The rock is also broken vertically by smaller cracks with no displacement visible. When the frequency of horizontal cracks is added to the fact of vertical cracks we have a climber's nightmare. In the introduction to the climbing guidebook of the southern Rockies Putnam and Boles comment 'basically this is not an area of sound rock and all routes are subject to rockfall in varying degrees of danger.' The lure of the peaks remain irresistible, partly because of the many 'mixed climbs' where rock, snow and ice can all be experienced in a single day's outing.

The Main Ranges are characterized by glaciation. Along the continental height of land or 'The Great Divide' winter snowfall outpaces summer melt and there is an accumulation of snow from one year to the next. The layers of snow compress the snow beneath and over a long period of time thick ice builds up. Under its own weight the ice moves slowly downhill like a frozen river, eroding layers of rock in its path.

By 1884 Lake Louise was linked to the valley by a rough wagon road and two years later the first small fisherman's cabin was built on the shore. Each subsequent building on the site has enjoyed the same view of the turquoise waters and the face and glacier of Mount Victoria beyond. So popular did the C.P.R. Hotel here become that in 1912 a cog railway was put in so guests could be met down at the main line and brought to the hotel with comfort and speed.

The common fate of wooden structures in the early days was fire and the first chalet, built in 1890, lasted only a year. The new and large building welcomed many more guests including the five enthusiasts of the Yale Lake Louise Club who came for several summers from 1894. They produced the first detailed map of the area. The photographs taken by Walter Wilcox at this time remain some of the finest of the region. His book Camping in the Canadian Rockies drew many to the mountains.

In 1884 Allen, Wilcox and Frissell, proud members of the Yale Lake Louise Club made the first ascent of Mount Temple, at 11,626 feet the highest peak in the area. Their route up the southwest face is today called the 'tourist route'.

(Preceding pages:) Mount Eisenhower 2,752m (9030 ft.) is probably the best example in Canada of a 'castellate' or castle mountain. The mountain was originally known as Castle Mountain, but was re-named after World War II. Mount Eisenhower offers one of the most spectacular sights in the park, and can be clearly seen from the highway between Banff and Lake Louise.

The awesome north wall of the mountain was not climbed until 1966 when Charlie Locke and Brian Greenwood of Calgary spent two days and a night solving the problems it posed.

The members of the Yale group were the explorers of the adjacent valleys frequently visited today, Paradise Valley and Valley of the Ten Peaks. From Mitre Pass they looked down on the beauty of Paradise Valley which they hurried to see at closer range. Today's trail follows beside the Giant Steps where water streams down over a huge staircase of quartzite beds.

Wilcox first likened the Valley of the Ten Peaks to 'a vale of desolation and death.' The Ten Peaks rise steeply, hemming in the valley; heaps of rock debris encircle the lake. Allen gave the ten peaks the names of Stony Indian numbers, but seven of them are today known by more recent names. The great pile of rock at the near end of the lake was at first thought to have been deposited there by glacial action, but is now known to be a rock slide. Above the end of the lake the movement of Wenkchemna Glacier can be seen where it has encroached on the forest.

Larch Valley above Moraine Lake is best visited in September. The Lyall's larch marks the division between coniferous forest below and tundra above. In autumn this deciduous conifer, Larix lyallii, changes from green to brilliant gold and its needles are swept to the ground in the first blizzards. In spring, feather-soft needles of brilliant green sprout again from the black, irregular branches. The distinctively ragged silhouette of the tree has caught the eye of painters and photographers.

The Yale Lake Louise Club was not the only group to come west in search of alpine adventure. In 1894 Charles Fay, a member of the Appalachian Mountain Club, brought a large party to Lake Louise including Philip Abbot who had climbed in the Swiss Alps. Mount Lefroy eluded them that year but they came west again the following summer and with Abbot leading, set out for the steep slopes. Uncertain of the route at the higher level he unroped to investigate alone. A small slip and his horrified friends, unable to help, watched him hurtle down the mountainside. Abbot's death was the first known mountaineering fatality in North America, and it raised many questions about the risks of the sport. But one year to the day after the accident Professor Fay, Norman Collie and the Swiss guide Peter Sarbach stood on the summit of Mount Lefroy.

Summer meetings of mountaineers and aspiring mountaineers took place in the Lake Louise area in the form of camps of the Alpine Club of Canada. Seven such camps were held in Paradise Valley, Consolation Valley and Larch Valley. Much work was done on trails and bridges at these times. The campsites were enormous by today's standards with about one hundred and fifty members staying for more than a week. Activities were strictly regimented and no climbing was done on Sundays. The Alpine Club of Canada thrives today, its character having changed over the years, like climbing itself.

The C.P.R. realized the wisdom of promoting the mountains and compared them to Switzerland with brochures such as 'Mountaineering in the Canadian Alps.' They

(Opposite) The poppies of Lake Louise are one of the better known sights of the area. (Above) The Chateau Lake Louise. (Below) Hikers set out in winter across the frozen surface of Lake Louise. The trip is a very popular trip for visitors in winter.

brought Swiss guides to Lake Louise where they enjoyed their own guides' chalet by the water's edge. In 1922 the guides built the stone alpine hut which still stands today high on Abbot Pass. The focus of climbing gradually shifted from the Selkirk Mountains where visitors stayed at Glacier House, to the Rockies where Chateau Lake Louise and the Alpine Clubhouse at Banff were bases for their outings.

From Lake Louise the outfitting enabled non-alpinists to experience something of the Rockies. Charles Walcott of the Smithsonian Institute made extensive geological studies and mapped many of the rock formations. William Scherzer studied and reported on the Victoria and Wenkchemna glaciers. Most of the early visitors, distinguished or otherwise could not have penetrated the wilderness without the advise and expertise of the packers and wranglers working out of Banff, Lake Louise and Field. One of this hearty corps, Ralph Edwards, itemized the factors in the opening up of the mountain terrain: the dudes, the guides and packers, the cooks and the Indian pony.

Summer visitors to Lake Louise are naturally drawn to the lake but some of the finest views of the area are from the north side of the Bow Valley on the slopes of Mount Whitehorn. The Gondola lift, almost four kilometres in length carries visitors up to an uninterrupted view of Lake Louise and the peaks along the Continental Divide.

The name Lake Louise has the added ring of skiing. The enthusiasm of the Ski Club of the Canadian Rockies saw Skoki Camp, Halfway Hut and Temple all active in the 30's. Skoki remains a favourite destination of cross-country skiers in the spring. Skiing in the Sunshine area began with the use of the Trail Riders' cabin for a ski camp in the 1930's. In the 1920's the Banff Ski Club organized skiing on Mount Norquay and built a small log cabin for warming up.

The packhorse is disappearing now, the automobile speeds today's visitor on his way, and only mountaineers camp under canvas. Changes of pace have occurred, and changes in park values as well. We used to think that taking care of the wildlife only meant prohibiting hunting, and that feeding the bears made good photographs!

A century ago when Banff National Park was created it covered only ten square miles. In the ensuing decades it grew and shrank before it settled to its present 6,641 square kilometres (2,564 square miles), a size we thought so enormous it must be "wilderness". The trip from Jasper to Banff in 1911 required thirteen days. Those were long days rich with the colours of fireweed and green lakes, full of the sound of wind in the pines and lake water washing against the shore.

Today the drive from Jasper to Banff takes only four hours. We cannot turn back, but must treasure what remains, not just for the sake of future generations, but for the wild beauty that is the Canadian Rockies.

(Opposite:) Mount Lefroy 3423m (11,230 ft.) as seen from Lake Louise. Following pages (Above left:) The Bow River east of Canmore with Chinaman's Peak to the left, and Mount Rundle in the background. (Below left:) Ox-eye daisies in flower. (Above right:) A colourful close-up. (Below right:) Mount Erasmus 3262m (10,700 ft.) in the northwestern corner of Banff National Park.

Preceding pages (Left:) An intrepid skier leaps into the air from Tipi Town Rock at the Sunshine Ski Area. (Above right:) Rocky Mountain Sheep such as this ram can be seen in many areas of the Rockies. During the summer the males associate in groups by themselves, whilst the females live with their young. (Below right:) Sunset over the Rockies.

(Right:) Cross-country skiers pause at a cabin for lunch. (Below:) The Crowfoot Glacier located near the southeastern end of Bow Lake. (Opposite:) Lake Louise: The glacier-covered Mount Victoria can be seen through the trees.

(Left:) Moraine Lake with some of the 'Ten Peaks' in background. The lake lies in a valley known as the Valley of the Ten Peaks. (Below:) Close-ups of plant life on the banks of the Vermilion Lakes. (Opposite:) A small stream tumbles over rocks on its way to a larger watershed.

Banff National Park contains many smaller rivers which flow into the two large rivers — the Bow and North Saskatchewan.

Following pages. (Left above:) Summer visitors relaxing on the shores of a lake. (Left below:) Mt. Wilson. (Right above:) A pair of Common Mergansers. (Right below:) This spectacular view is from the north face of Mount Assiniboine looking across the Purcell Range in British Columbia.

(Above left:) Bunchberries. (Above right:) The wild rose — the provincial flower of Alberta. (Below:) Banff with Cascade Mountain in the background. (Opposite:) Mount Assiniboine 3,630m (11,870 feet) is the tallest mountain in the park.

"Winter in Banff"

"Communal plant life"